Renovating Trust

Self-help Tips and Strategies to Reestablish Love, Trust, and Closeness in Your Relationship

By

Linda J. Williams

Table of Contents

introduction

In the complicated tapestry of human relationships, the threads of love, trust, and emotional proximity weave a bond that defines the very essence of intimate connections. These vital qualities serve as the cornerstone of a good and satisfying relationship, generating a sense of security, understanding, and emotional support between couples. Love covers the strong affection, admiration, and emotional attachment that bonds persons, producing a shared sense of intimacy and friendship. Trust, on the other hand, represents the underlying belief in the reliability, honesty, and integrity of one's partner, forming the foundations upon which the relationship develops and flourishes. Lastly, emotional intimacy symbolizes the personal connection that surpasses physical proximity, generating a profound understanding and empathy between couples and developing a sense of belonging and mutual admiration.

While these pillars are the cornerstone of a successful and long relationship, they are not impervious to the obstacles and complexities that life inevitably presents. Miscommunication, unresolved disagreements, breaches of trust, and the demands of daily life can all contribute to the slow erosion of these important qualities, generating tension and discord within the relationship. As a result, the need to remodel and revitalize the foundation of love, trust, and proximity becomes imperative, signaling a demand for introspection, understanding, and conscious attempts to rebuild the emotional connection and intimacy that may have been damaged over time.

The process of renovating trust and reestablishing love and closeness within a relationship requires a holistic approach that encompasses effective communication strategies, the cultivation of empathy and understanding, the demonstration of accountability and transparency, and the allocation of quality time for shared activities and experiences. Moreover, it entails the active practice of conflict resolution techniques that foster constructive dialogue and mutual respect, the regular expression of appreciation and affection, and the recognition of the significance of self-care and personal growth in nurturing the well-being of the relationship. Additionally, the role of external support through professional counseling or therapy can provide essential direction and insights, allowing the rebuilding of trust and emotional connection in times of struggle and uncertainty.

By delving into these self-help suggestions and tactics, individuals can start on a transforming journey of reflection, growth, and relationship restoration, cultivating a deeper awareness of their wants and desires, as well as those of their partner. Through the implementation of these effective techniques, couples can navigate the intricate terrain of relationship dynamics, rekindling the flame of love, fostering mutual trust, and cultivating emotional closeness, thereby laying the groundwork for a more resilient, fulfilling, and enduring connection with their significant other.

It is through these intentional and dedicated efforts that the foundations of love, trust, and closeness can be strengthened and fortified, fostering a relationship that withstands the tests of time and adversity and blossoms into a source of joy, companionship, and mutual growth for both partners involved.

Chapter 1

Understanding the Foundations of Love and Trust

Love and trust are the primary building blocks of good and happy partnerships. Each plays a key role in building emotional closeness, fostering a sense of security, and nurturing a profound connection between persons. To establish a strong and durable link, it is vital to know the subtle dynamics and foundations of love and trust within the framework of a relationship.

Love, in its essence, is a multidimensional and intense emotional bond that surpasses mere infatuation or physical attraction. It comprises a complicated combination of affection, admiration, respect, and a genuine desire for the well-being and happiness of one's partner. Love thrives on true caring, empathy, and the willingness to prioritize the needs and happiness of the other individual. It forms the emotional substrate upon which a relationship grows and evolves, providing a sense of belonging, support, and companionship that is necessary for personal and mutual progress.

Trust, on the other hand, acts as the cornerstone of a healthy and successful partnership. It is the steadfast belief in the reliability, honesty, and integrity of one's relationship. Trust comprises a sense of comfort and confidence that enables individuals to be vulnerable, open, and authentic within the connection. It is cultivated via regular acts, open communication, and the demonstration of dependability and accountability. Trust is not just formed on words but is solidified by the alignment of actions with pledges, establishing a secure and supportive environment where both partners may express themselves freely without fear of criticism or betrayal.

The interplay between love and trust generates a symbiotic relationship, as the existence of one often encourages the growth and development of the other. Love without trust can be weak and quickly shattered by doubt, uneasiness, and uncertainty. Conversely, trust without love may produce a sense of emotional detachment and distance, missing the depth and emotional connection that supports a fulfilling and meaningful relationship. Therefore, understanding and nurturing both love and trust are crucial for establishing a relationship that is robust, authentic, and founded on a strong foundation of mutual respect, understanding, and emotional security.

To strengthen the foundations of love and trust within a relationship, it is vital to establish open and honest communication, foster empathy and understanding, and prioritize the demonstration of reliability and accountability. Creating a secure and non-judgmental environment for expressing emotions, worries, and wants helps promote a deeper understanding of each other's views and facilitates the development of mutual empathy and emotional connection. Moreover, intentionally exhibiting integrity, consistency, and transparency in one's activities can enhance the trust between partners, generating a sense of security and emotional well-being inside the partnership.

By acknowledging the value of love and trust as the core of a good relationship, individuals may embark on a journey of self-reflection, growth, and mutual understanding, building an environment of emotional security, respect, and true connection. Through the fostering of these core characteristics, couples can cultivate a relationship that is built on mutual respect, understanding, and a deep emotional bond that withstands the tests of time and adversity.

Exploring the components of love and trust in a relationship

Exploring the components of love and trust in a relationship means delving into the numerous factors that constitute the essence of these foundational pillars. Understanding the complex nature of love and trust is vital for developing a deep and meaningful connection within the context of a relationship.

Love, as a complex and dynamic emotion, involves different components that contribute to the depth and closeness of a relationship. These components often include:

1. Affection: Affection is the basis of love, encompassing feelings of warmth, tenderness, and fondness for one's partner. Expressions of affection, such as physical touch, verbal affirmations, and acts of kindness, play a crucial role in establishing emotional closeness and strengthening the link between couples.

2. Respect: Respect is a crucial component of love that requires acknowledging and honoring the views, opinions, and boundaries of one's partner. It requires respecting each other with dignity, honoring one other's opinions, and building an environment of mutual admiration and consideration.

3.   Understanding: Understanding   entails empathizing with and grasping the feelings, experiences, and wants of one's partner. It demands active listening, empathy, and the willingness to acknowledge and affirm the thoughts and viewpoints of the other individual, generating a sense of emotional connection and mutual support.

4. Support: Support is a key facet of love that comprises providing emotional, mental, and physical support to one's spouse at times of need or difficulties. Offering encouragement, reassurance, and practical support develops a sense of security and trust, deepening the emotional tie and maintaining the foundation of the relationship.

Trust, as the core of a good relationship, involves numerous critical components that establish a sense of security, reliability, and emotional safety. These components often include:

1. Reliability: Reliability forms the cornerstone of trust, comprising the continuous and dependable behavior of one's partner. It involves honoring agreements, being consistent in actions, and displaying a feeling of dependability and accountability that provides a secure and stable atmosphere inside the partnership.

2. Honesty: Honesty is a vital component of trust that comprises open and straightforward communication, devoid of fraud or concealment. It comprises sharing one's thoughts, feelings, and experiences authentically, generating a sense of honesty and integrity that enhances the emotional link and promotes a deeper level of trust.

3. Consistency: Consistency is vital for creating and keeping trust since it includes aligning actions with words and maintaining a predictable and stable tone within the partnership. Consistent behavior promotes a sense of emotional stability and reliability, laying the framework for a stable and durable commitment between partners.

4. Vulnerability: Vulnerability is a vital component of trust that requires the willingness to be honest, sincere, and authentic with one's relationship. It comprises discussing worries, insecurities, and feelings without fear of judgment or betrayal, building a sense of emotional intimacy and mutual understanding within the partnership.

By recognizing and fostering these components of love and trust, individuals can cultivate a relationship that is founded on a strong foundation of mutual respect, understanding, and emotional security. Emphasizing the value of compassion, respect, understanding, and support, alongside reliability, honesty, consistency, and vulnerability, can develop an environment of emotional intimacy, authenticity, and trust that enhances the bond and resilience of the relationship over time.

Analyzing the impact of trust on the overall health of a relationship

Analyzing the impact of trust on the entire health of a relationship requires recognizing the tremendous influence that trust exerts on the emotional well-being, stability, and durability of a partnership. Trust acts as a vital element that underpins the cornerstone of a healthy and happy relationship, considerably affecting numerous areas of the partnership dynamics.

1. Emotional Security: Trust generates a sense of emotional security inside a relationship, allowing individuals to feel protected, supported, and understood by their partners. A high level of trust cultivates an environment where individuals may openly communicate their thoughts, feelings, and weaknesses without fear of judgment or betrayal, encouraging emotional intimacy and mutual understanding.

2. conversation: Trust plays a crucial role in allowing open and honest conversation between partners. A strong foundation of trust empowers individuals to communicate their ideas, problems and wants without hesitation, promoting an atmosphere of transparency, empathy, and mutual respect. Effective communication, founded on a foundation of trust, enables the settlement of problems, the expression of affection, and the cultivation of a deeper emotional connection.

3. Intimacy: Trust is vital for creating emotional and physical intimacy within a partnership. A high level of trust enables individuals to be vulnerable and sincere with their partners, offering a space for genuine emotional connection and mutual understanding. Trust encourages the formation of a strong emotional link, establishing a sense of intimacy and companionship that is vital for sustaining a successful and meaningful partnership.

4. Stability: Trust adds to the general stability of a relationship, giving a sturdy foundation that withstands the obstacles and uncertainties of daily life. A high level of trust develops a sense of reliability, consistency, and predictability within the relationship, establishing an environment where individuals can depend on and rely on their partners for support, understanding, and companionship.

5. Mutual Respect: Trust is intimately entwined with mutual respect, forming the bedrock of a healthy and respectful connection. Trust helps individuals honor one another's boundaries, opinions, and viewpoints, generating an environment of mutual admiration, consideration, and support. Mutual respect, built on trust, develops an atmosphere of understanding and appreciation, developing a deep and enduring tie between couples.

6. Conflict settlement: Trust enables efficient conflict settlement within a partnership. A high level of trust helps individuals to participate in constructive discourse, empathy, and compromise, enabling the settlement of problems in a manner that respects each other's perspectives and develops a sense of mutual understanding and reconciliation. Trust-based conflict resolution enhances the emotional tie between partners, establishing an atmosphere of emotional resilience and cooperation.

By realizing the tremendous impact of trust on the overall health of a relationship, individuals may prioritize the creation of a strong foundation of trust, transparency, and emotional security within their connection. Fostering open communication, mutual respect, stability, and intimacy based on trust can produce an environment that supports emotional well-being, understanding, and long-term fulfillment within the partnership.

Chapter 2

Identifying the Challenges in Your Relationship

Identifying the obstacles in your relationship is a vital step in understanding the underlying dynamics and addressing the concerns that may be inhibiting the growth and well-being of the partnership. Recognizing and accepting the specific issues that affect your relationship can provide significant insights and assistance for applying successful techniques to overcome obstacles and create a stronger and more fulfilling connection with your partner.

1. Communication Breakdown: Communication problems can greatly damage the quality of a relationship. Issues such as misconceptions, misinterpretations, and a lack of efficient communication can lead to confrontations, emotional distance, and a sense of separation between partners.

2. Trust concerns: Trust concerns, including breaches of trust, dishonesty, or past betrayals, can constitute a substantial obstacle to the formation of a healthy and strong relationship. Overcoming trust issues requires rebuilding trust via transparency, consistency, and open communication.

3. Emotional Distance: Emotional distance can emerge due to several circumstances, such as busy schedules, personal stress, or unresolved problems. It can lead to a sense of separation, loneliness, and a lack of emotional connection within the partnership.

4. Conflicting Priorities: Conflicting priorities and goals between partners can produce stress and strife inside the partnership. Differences in values, life aspirations, or job ambitions may lead to difficulty in establishing common ground and fostering a sense of mutual understanding and support.

5. connection Issues: Intimacy issues, especially a lack of physical or emotional connection, can damage the overall health of the relationship. Factors such as stress, weariness, or unsolved problems can contribute to a drop in intimacy, leading to feelings of dissatisfaction and detachment between partners.

6. External Stressors: External stressors, such as financial issues, work-related stress, or family pressures, can have a substantial impact on the relationship dynamics. Managing external stressors involves good communication, mutual support, and a collaborative strategy to navigate through hard circumstances together.

7. Unresolved disagreements: Unresolved disagreements and frequent arguments can create a cycle of negativity and emotional strain inside the relationship. Failure to discuss and resolve disagreements constructively can lead to resentment, emotional distance, and a breakdown in communication between partners.

8. Lack of Quality Time: A lack of quality time spent together can lead to feelings of neglect, isolation, and emotional separation. Busy schedules, personal commitments, or other responsibilities may inhibit the formation of a deep emotional link and shared experiences between couples.

By identifying and comprehending these problems, individuals can obtain vital insights into the precise areas that demand attention and progress within their relationship. Addressing these problems through effective communication, trust-building measures, conflict resolution approaches, and the priority of quality time can help establish a stronger, more resilient, and meaningful partnership that withstands the tests of time and hardship.

Recognizing frequent obstacles that lead to a breakdown of trust and love

Recognizing frequent issues that lead to a breakdown of trust and love is vital for understanding the elements that can affect the health and sustainability of a relationship. Identifying these problems can provide valuable insights into the specific areas that require focus and resolution, allowing individuals to execute effective techniques for rebuilding trust and establishing a deeper sense of love and connection within their partnership.

1. Communication Breakdown: Communication issues, such as misunderstandings, misinterpretations, and a lack of productive discourse, can lead to a breakdown of trust and emotional intimacy. Poor communication may result in emotions of neglect, irritation, and a sense of emotional detachment between spouses.

2. Infidelity and Betrayal: Infidelity and breaches of trust can have a devastating influence on the foundation of a partnership. Acts of betrayal, whether emotional or physical, can lead to emotions of insecurity, betrayal, and a severe erosion of trust and emotional connection between partners.

3. Lack of Transparency: A lack of transparency in expressing thoughts, feelings, and experiences might limit the development of trust and emotional closeness within the relationship. Secrets, hidden intentions, and a lack of candor can lead to emotions of distrust, uncertainty, and a breakdown in the emotional link between partners.

4. Unresolved Conflicts: Unresolved conflicts and frequent fights can create a cycle of negativity and emotional strain, leading to a reduction in love and trust. Failure to address and resolve disagreements constructively can result in resentment, emotional distance, and a breakdown of effective communication between partners.

5. Neglect and Indifference: Neglect and indifference can result in a slow erosion of affection and trust within the partnership. Emotional neglect, a lack of affection, or a failure to prioritize the needs and well-being of one's spouse can lead to feelings of separation, loneliness, and a sense of emotional detachment.

6. Incompatibility and mismatched Expectations: Incompatibility and mismatched expectations between partners can create substantial problems in building a deep and meaningful connection. Differences in values, life goals, or relationship expectations may lead to disputes, misunderstandings, and a lack of emotional resonance and understanding.

7. External stresses: External stresses, such as financial obligations, work-related challenges, or family duties, can strain the relationship and lead to emotional tiredness and a breakdown in communication and emotional support. Managing external stressors properly is vital for establishing resilience and maintaining a strong emotional tie within the relationship.

By recognizing these frequent issues, individuals can obtain a greater knowledge of the elements that can contribute to a breakdown of trust and love within their relationship. Addressing these challenges through effective communication, trust-building strategies, conflict resolution techniques, and the cultivation of mutual understanding and emotional support can help rebuild trust and foster a deeper sense of love and connection, strengthening the foundation of the relationship and promoting long-term emotional well-being and fulfillment.

Assessing the precise issues affecting your relationship dynamics

Assessing the exact difficulties influencing your relationship dynamics is a vital step in identifying the fundamental reasons for any obstacles or tensions within the partnership. By conducting a comprehensive assessment, individuals can gain valuable insights into the specific areas that require attention, resolution, and potential improvement, allowing for the implementation of targeted strategies to address the issues and foster a healthier and more fulfilling connection with their partner.

1. Communication Patterns: Assess the communication patterns within the relationship, including the frequency, quality, and efficacy of communication between partners. Evaluate whether there are any impediments to open and honest discourse and identify any communication patterns or styles that may contribute to misunderstandings or conflicts.

2. Trust and Intimacy Levels: Evaluate the current levels of trust and intimacy within the partnership. Assess the degree of emotional closeness, vulnerability, and transparency between partners and identify any reasons hindering the development of trust and emotional intimacy, such as prior betrayals, unresolved conflicts, or communication challenges.

3. Emotional Connection: Assess the strength of the emotional connection between partners, including empathy, understanding, and mutual support. Evaluate whether there are any hurdles to building a deep and meaningful emotional attachment, such as emotional distance, unsolved issues, or unfulfilled emotional needs.

4. Shared Goals and Values: Assess the alignment of shared goals, values, and aspirations amongst partners. Evaluate whether substantial differences or conflicts in values, life objectives, or relationship expectations may contribute to misunderstandings or tensions within the partnership.

5. Time Spent Together: Assess the quality and quantity of time spent together as a couple. Evaluate whether there are any constraints or external circumstances that may be inhibiting the allocation of quality time for shared activities, conversations, and emotional connection, such as work commitments, family responsibilities, or personal priorities.

6. Conflict Resolution tactics: Assess the effectiveness of conflict resolution tactics within the relationship. Evaluate if disagreements are addressed productively and politely and identify any repeating patterns or communication styles that may escalate conflicts or misunderstandings.

7. External stresses: Assess the impact of external stresses on the relationship dynamics. Evaluate whether external issues, such as financial pressures, work-related challenges, or family duties, strain the partnership's emotional well-being and stability.

By completing a thorough assessment of these specific difficulties, individuals can obtain a deeper understanding of the dynamics and obstacles inside their relationship. This examination can be a foundation for adopting focused techniques, developing open communication, repairing trust, nurturing emotional intimacy, and fostering a stronger and more resilient connection with their spouse.

Chapter 3

Effective Communication Strategies for Rebuilding Trust

Effective communication tactics are vital for regaining trust within a relationship. Open and honest communication forms the bedrock of a successful partnership. It acts as a critical tool for healing past breaches of trust and creating a deeper emotional connection and understanding between partners. By employing good communication practices, individuals may create a safe and supportive atmosphere that supports transparency, empathy, and mutual respect, laying the framework for repairing trust and strengthening the emotional link within the partnership.

1. Create a Safe and Non-Judgmental atmosphere: Foster a safe and non-judgmental atmosphere for open communication and emotional expression. Encourage your partner to share their thoughts, feelings, and worries without fear of criticism or punishment, and display active listening and empathy to create a deeper understanding of their perspective.

2. Practice Active Listening: Practice active listening by giving your partner your complete attention and exhibiting genuine interest in their views and experiences. Listen without interrupting, validate their emotions, and ask clarifying questions to thoroughly understand their perspective before reacting.

3. Express Yourself Honestly and plainly: Express yourself honestly and plainly, sharing your thoughts, feelings, and experiences transparently and authentically. Avoid withholding information or disguising your emotions, as this might inhibit the development of trust and emotional closeness within the partnership.

4. Validate Your Partner's Feelings: Validate your partner's feelings and experiences by acknowledging the validity of their emotions and exhibiting empathy and compassion. Avoid ignoring or discounting their problems, and show compassion and support for their emotional well-being and perspective.

5. Be Accountable for Your acts: Take responsibility for your acts and decisions, exhibiting accountability and integrity in your behavior.

Acknowledge any prior mistakes or breaches of trust, and demonstrate your resolve to restore trust via consistent and reliable behaviors and clear communication.

6. Foster Empathy and Understanding: Cultivate empathy and understanding by putting yourself in your partner's shoes and acknowledging the influence of your words and actions on their emotions and well-being. Demonstrate a genuine desire to understand their perspective and show compassion and support for their experiences and worries.

7. Practice Patience and Respect: Practice patience and respect in your communication, offering your partner the time and space to express themselves without feeling rushed or forced. Avoid leaping to conclusions or making assumptions, and develop an environment of mutual respect and regard for each other's opinions and feelings.

8. Set Clear Expectations and Boundaries: Set clear expectations and boundaries for communication within the partnership, creating standards for respectful and constructive discourse. Communicate frankly about your needs and preferences, and urge your spouse to do the same, building a climate of mutual understanding and respect.

By using these successful communication tactics, individuals can set the framework for regaining trust within their relationships. Creating a safe and supportive space for open dialogue, practicing active listening, expressing oneself honestly and transparently, fostering empathy and understanding, and demonstrating accountability and respect can contribute to the development of a stronger and more resilient emotional connection, fostering trust, and strengthening the foundation of the relationship.

Emphasizing the significance of open and honest communication

Emphasizing the significance of open and honest communication is vital for creating a healthy and happy relationship. Open and honest communication serves as the cornerstone of a strong emotional link, promoting trust, understanding, and mutual respect between partners. By promoting truthful and real discourse, individuals may establish a safe and supportive environment that supports vulnerability, empathy, and a deeper connection within the partnership.

1. Fosters Trust and Emotional Intimacy: Open and honest communication develops trust and emotional closeness by offering a secure space for individuals to communicate their thoughts, feelings, and worries without fear of judgment or rejection. It helps partners to be vulnerable and real with each other, establishing a deeper sense of emotional closeness and understanding.

2. Resolves Misunderstandings and arguments: Open and honest communication helps to overcome misunderstandings and disputes by allowing individuals to address issues and concerns productively and courteously. It fosters active listening, empathy, and the explanation of intentions, establishing a climate of mutual understanding and cooperation.

3. Develop a Foundation of Transparency and Integrity: Open and honest communication develops a foundation of transparency and integrity inside the connection. It encourages individuals to express their thoughts and experiences truthfully, providing an environment of trust, trustworthiness, and dependability that enhances the emotional tie and promotes a stronger sense of connection and mutual respect.

4.   increases   Emotional   Support   and Understanding: Open and honest communication increases emotional support and understanding by creating a platform for individuals to express their needs, worries, and emotions openly. It encourages empathy, compassion, and active listening, allowing partners to provide each other with the emotional validation, encouragement, and support needed to navigate through challenges and tough circumstances.

5. fosters Personal Growth and Mutual Respect: Open and honest communication fosters personal growth and mutual respect by encouraging individuals to articulate their values, objectives, and boundaries within the partnership. It develops an atmosphere of mutual respect, understanding, and consideration, allowing partners to encourage each other's personal development and foster a sense of shared growth and fulfillment.

6. improves the Emotional Relationship and Connection: Open and honest communication improves the emotional relationship and connection between partners by building a deep feeling of understanding, empathy, and shared experiences. It enables individuals to share their pleasures, sufferings, and goals, establishing a shared narrative that connects them and develops a stronger sense of emotional resonance and connection.

By emphasizing the significance of open and honest communication within the relationship, individuals can develop a robust emotional link that withstands the challenges of time and adversity. Prioritizing transparent discourse, active listening, and empathy develops a climate of trust, emotional closeness, and mutual understanding, cultivating a relationship that is founded on a foundation of transparency, respect, and true connection.

Discussing approaches for active listening and creating empathy

Discussing skills for active listening and cultivating empathy can dramatically boost the quality of communication and understanding within a relationship. Active listening and empathy serve as key tools for creating a caring and loving atmosphere that encourages emotional connection and mutual understanding between couples. By using these approaches, individuals can display real interest in their partner's ideas and feelings, building a stronger sense of empathy, compassion, and emotional resonance within the connection.

1. Practice Active Listening: Actively listen to your spouse by giving them your entire attention and focusing on their words and nonverbal signs. Avoid distractions, such as electronic gadgets or external stimuli, and display real interest in what they are saying by maintaining eye contact and nodding to signal your understanding and participation.

2. Reflective Responses: Provide reflective responses to illustrate your knowledge and validate your partner's feelings and experiences. Paraphrase their statements to reinforce your comprehension and reflect their emotions, showing that you are actively engaged and attentive to their perspective and emotional state.

3. Ask Open-Ended inquiries: Ask open-ended inquiries to encourage your partner to elaborate on their views and feelings. Avoid closed-ended inquiries that elicit simple "yes" or "no" replies, and instead, ask probing questions that promote deeper contemplation and urge your partner to share more about their experiences, viewpoints, and emotional needs.

4. Validate Emotions: Validate your partner's emotions by acknowledging the reality of their feelings and experiences without judgment or criticism. Show empathy and compassion for their emotional state, and communicate your support and understanding for their perspective, building a sense of emotional safety and mutual trust within the connection.

5. Demonstrate Empathy: Demonstrate empathy by putting yourself in your partner's shoes and striving to comprehend their perspective and experiences from their point of view. Acknowledge their feelings, experiences, and struggles, and offer compassion and support for their emotional well-being, establishing a stronger connection and understanding within the partnership.

6. Nonverbal Communication: Pay attention to nonverbal indicators, such as facial expressions, gestures, and body language, to obtain a deeper understanding of your partner's feelings and experiences. Be alert to their nonverbal cues to uncover any underlying feelings or concerns that may not be openly articulated, and respond with empathy and compassion to develop a deeper emotional connection and mutual understanding.

7. Create a friendly setting: Create a friendly and non-judgmental setting that supports open and honest conversation, vulnerability, and emotional expression. Foster a climate of trust and emotional safety, where your spouse feels comfortable discussing their thoughts, feelings, and concerns without fear of criticism or rejection, generating a greater sense of emotional connection and mutual understanding within the partnership.

By discussing and practicing these tactics for active listening and building empathy, individuals may establish a supportive and loving environment that creates a stronger feeling of emotional connection, understanding, and mutual respect within the relationship. Prioritizing active listening, reflective responses, open-ended inquiries, validation of emotions, and nonverbal communication can dramatically boost the quality of communication and empathy, establishing a stronger and more resilient emotional link between partners.

Chapter 4

Rebuilding Trust Through Transparency and Accountability

Rebuilding trust via transparency and accountability is vital for developing a stronger and more resilient bond within a partnership. Transparency and accountability serve as key components for exhibiting integrity, dependability, and trustworthiness, building a firm foundation upon which trust may be reestablished and emotional closeness can be maintained. By prioritizing these qualities, individuals can build a supportive and trusting environment that supports open communication, vulnerability, and mutual understanding within the partnership.

1. Open and Transparent Communication: Foster open and transparent communication by discussing your views, feelings, and experiences openly and honestly with your partner. Avoid withholding information or concealing key details, as this might impair the development of trust and emotional intimacy within the partnership. Demonstrate a desire to be vulnerable and real, promoting a climate of mutual transparency and understanding.

2. Consistent and Reliable Behavior: Demonstrate consistent and reliable behavior to create trust and foster a sense of emotional stability inside the connection. Align your actions with your words and commitments, and follow through on your pledges to demonstrate your reliability and integrity. Consistent and reliable behavior supports the concept that you can be counted on and trusted, offering a stable and supportive atmosphere for establishing emotional connection and understanding.

3. Honesty and Integrity: Prioritize honesty and integrity in all parts of your relationship, exhibiting a dedication to truthfulness and ethical behavior. Avoid deceit, manipulation, or dishonesty, as these can weaken the foundation of trust and compromise the emotional relationship between spouses. Emphasize the importance of ethical conduct and moral principles, generating a sense of mutual respect and integrity within the relationship.

4. Demonstrate Vulnerability and Openness: Demonstrate vulnerability and openness by communicating your anxieties, insecurities, and concerns with your spouse. Create a safe and supportive space for expressing your emotions and experiences without fear of judgment or criticism, building a greater emotional connection and understanding. Encourage your partner to do the same, building an atmosphere of reciprocal vulnerability and empathy.

5. Take Responsibility for Your Actions: Take responsibility for your actions and decisions, acknowledge any prior mistakes or breaches of trust, and display a true commitment to reform and progress. Avoid shifting responsibility or making excuses, and take aggressive measures to repair any prior faults and rebuild trust via consistent and trustworthy behavior. Take responsibility for your role in the relationship and display accountability for your actions, generating a sense of mutual respect and understanding within the partnership.

6. Cultivate Mutual Understanding and Empathy: Cultivate mutual understanding and empathy by exhibiting compassion and support for your partner's experiences, feelings, and obstacles. Show real interest in their well-being and actively listen to their problems and wants, building a greater emotional connection and trust within the partnership. Demonstrate empathy and compassion in times of difficulty and uncertainty, and offer your support and encouragement to develop an environment of mutual understanding and emotional resilience within the relationship.

By concentrating on restoring trust via openness and responsibility, individuals may create a supportive and trusting environment that supports open communication, vulnerability, and mutual understanding within the relationship. Prioritizing open and transparent communication, consistent and trustworthy conduct, honesty and integrity, vulnerability and openness, and mutual understanding and empathy can considerably strengthen the quality of the emotional link and develop a stronger and more robust relationship between partners.

Highlighting the relevance of openness in repairing trust

Highlighting the significance of transparency in regaining trust is vital for developing a strong and resilient emotional tie within a partnership.

Transparency acts as a critical aspect in developing openness, honesty, and accountability, creating a foundation of mutual understanding and respect that allows partners to develop a stronger feeling of trust and emotional connection. By emphasizing the importance of transparency, individuals can establish a supportive and loving environment that supports open communication, vulnerability, and mutual progress within the partnership.

1. Fostering Open Communication: Transparency supports open communication by offering a safe and non-judgmental space for individuals to share their views, feelings, and concerns openly. It promotes partners to communicate vital information and experiences without fear of criticism or punishment, generating a greater sense of emotional connection and mutual understanding within the partnership.

2. Building Trust via Honesty: Transparency fosters trust via honesty and integrity, exhibiting a commitment to truthfulness and ethical conduct within the connection. It encourages individuals to be honest and authentic in their relationships, generating an environment of mutual trust and respect that enhances the emotional bond and develops a deeper feeling of emotional connection and understanding.

3. Demonstrating Reliability and Consistency: Transparency helps individuals to display reliability and consistency in their words and actions, matching their behavior with their commitments and pledges. It provides a sense of reliability and accountability, creating a secure and supportive environment for establishing emotional connection and understanding within the partnership.

4. Encouraging Mutual Understanding and Empathy: Transparency enhances mutual understanding and empathy by creating a forum for partners to communicate their viewpoints, experiences, and feelings openly. It develops an environment of reciprocal vulnerability and support, allowing individuals to express compassion and empathy for each other's experiences and struggles, developing a greater feeling of emotional connection and trust within the partnership.

5. Creating a Safe and Supportive Environment:
Transparency creates a safe and supportive environment that enables open communication, vulnerability, and emotional expression. It generates a climate of trust and emotional safety, where participants feel comfortable sharing their thoughts, feelings, and worries without fear of judgment or rejection, generating a greater sense of emotional connection and mutual understanding within the partnership.

6. Prioritizing Mutual Growth and Development:
Transparency prioritizes mutual growth and development within the partnership by allowing partners to discuss their aims, goals, and values openly. It develops an environment of mutual respect and understanding, allowing individuals to support each other's personal and professional progress and developing a greater sense of emotional connection and fulfillment within the relationship.

By recognizing the significance of transparency in repairing trust, individuals may establish a supportive and loving environment that supports open communication, vulnerability, and mutual progress within the relationship. Prioritizing open and transparent communication, honesty and integrity, reliability and consistency, mutual understanding and empathy, and creating a safe and supportive environment can significantly enhance the quality of the emotional bond and foster a stronger and more resilient connection between partners.

Outlining strategies for proving accountability and reliability

Outlining tactics for displaying accountability and reliability is vital for establishing a deeper sense of trust and emotional security within a partnership. Accountability and reliability serve as core characteristics that assist in the creation of a stable and supportive environment, enabling open communication, mutual understanding, and a deeper emotional link between partners. By following these tactics, individuals can demonstrate their commitment to ethical conduct and dependable behavior, building a sense of mutual trust and respect within the partnership.

1. Fulfill Commitments and Promises: Demonstrate accountability and reliability by meeting your commitments and promises to your partner. Prioritize follow-through on your words and actions, and ensure that you deliver on any agreements or duties that you have made, building a sense of reliability and integrity within the connection.

2. Be Transparent and Open: Demonstrate accountability and reliability by being transparent and open in your communication and actions. Avoid withholding information or concealing key data, and communicate openly and honestly with your spouse to build an environment of trust and mutual understanding within the relationship.

3. Take Ownership of Mistakes: Demonstrate accountability by taking ownership of your mistakes and addressing any errors or oversights that may have occurred. Avoid shifting blame or making excuses, and take aggressive steps to repair any previous faults and prevent similar occurrences in the future, building a sense of mutual respect and understanding within the relationship.

4.   Communicate   Expectations   Clearly: Communicate your expectations to your partner and urge them to do the same. Establish a shared awareness of each other's needs, boundaries, and objectives, and create an open discussion about your mutual goals and beliefs, building an atmosphere of transparency and reliability inside the partnership.

5. Follow Consistent and Ethical Practices: Demonstrate accountability and reliability by sticking to consistent and ethical practices in your interactions and decision-making processes. Prioritize ethical conduct and moral ideals in your acts, and ensure that your behavior matches with your personal and common principles, establishing a sense of mutual trust and respect within the partnership.

6. Cultivate a Supportive and Respectful Environment: Foster a supportive and respectful environment that supports open communication, empathy, and mutual understanding. Demonstrate respect for your partner's ideas, experiences, and feelings, and build an environment of trust and emotional safety that allows for open communication and vulnerability within the partnership.

7. Prioritize Emotional Support and empathy: Demonstrate accountability and reliability by prioritizing emotional support and empathy for your partner's experiences and struggles. Show empathy and compassion for their emotional well-being, and actively listen to their problems and needs to develop a deeper feeling of emotional connection and trust within the partnership.

By establishing and applying these tactics for displaying accountability and reliability, individuals can develop a deeper sense of trust and emotional security within their relationship. Prioritizing open communication, transparency, ownership of mistakes, clear expectations, consistent and ethical practices, a supportive environment, and emotional support and understanding can significantly enhance the quality of the emotional bond and foster a stronger and more resilient connection between partners.

Chapter 5

Cultivating Emotional Intimacy and Understanding

Cultivating emotional closeness and understanding is a vital component of building strong, healthy relationships, whether they are romantic, familial, or platonic. Emotional intimacy refers to the profound connection and understanding that individuals share, enabling them to communicate and empathize successfully with one another. Nurturing emotional closeness takes sincere efforts to create a secure and supportive environment where individuals feel comfortable expressing their thoughts and vulnerabilities without fear of judgment or rejection. Here are some crucial characteristics that might contribute to building emotional connection and understanding:

1. Effective Communication: Open and honest communication creates the cornerstone of emotional connection. Active listening, expressing oneself clearly, and being empathic are key components in building a deeper understanding of one another's feelings and experiences.

2. Empathy and Compassion: Developing empathy and compassion allows individuals to connect with others on a deeper level. Understanding and sharing in someone else's experiences can deepen emotional relationships and foster a sense of mutual support and understanding.

3. Vulnerability and Trust: Being able to be vulnerable and trusting others with your feelings is crucial for creating an emotional connection. When both partners feel confident in exposing their weaknesses without the fear of being ridiculed or judged, it provides the path for a deeper emotional connection.

4. Respect for Boundaries: Respecting each other's boundaries and emotional limits is vital for developing a healthy emotional relationship. Understanding when to provide space and when to provide assistance is vital for sustaining a balanced and respectful relationship.

5. Validation and Support: Providing emotional validation and support is crucial to building understanding. Validating someone's emotions and offering support during tough times helps individuals feel heard and understood, enhancing the emotional relationship between them.

6. Shared events: Sharing meaningful events and building enduring memories together can increase emotional connection. Whether it's through common hobbies, trips, or simply spending quality time together, these shared moments can build an emotional connection between individuals.

7. Conflict Resolution: Handling problems with compassion, empathy, and understanding is vital for preserving emotional connection. Resolving disagreements healthily and constructively allows individuals to discuss their differences while still respecting each other's emotions and opinions.

Cultivating emotional closeness and understanding is an ongoing process that needs effort, patience, and a willingness to connect profoundly with others. By prioritizing efficient communication, empathy, trust, and mutual respect, individuals can develop and maintain meaningful and fulfilling relationships based on emotional connection and understanding.

Discussing the significance of emotional intimacy in relationships

Emotional intimacy plays a critical part in creating healthy and fulfilling relationships. It involves the intimate connection, trust, and understanding that individuals share with their partners, friends, or family members. Here are some major features of emotional closeness in relationships:

1. Building Trust: Emotional closeness is built upon trust. When individuals feel comfortable and secure in expressing their thoughts, feelings, and weaknesses, they are more likely to create a deeper sense of trust in their relationships. This trust lays the foundation for open and honest conversation.

2. Enhancing conversation: Emotional intimacy facilitates effective and open conversation. It allows individuals to communicate their emotions, wants, and desires without the fear of criticism or rejection. This open discourse builds understanding and empathy, establishing a deeper connection between individuals.

3. Creating Empathy: Emotional intimacy develops empathy as individuals attempt to understand and relate to one another's emotions and experiences. Through empathy, people can build a better awareness of their partner's perspective, fostering a stronger emotional link and a sense of mutual support.

4. Fostering Support: Emotional closeness fosters a supportive environment where individuals feel comfortable seeking counsel, comfort, and encouragement from their relationships. This support system can considerably strengthen the relationship, especially during hard times.

5. Promoting Physical Intimacy: Emotional intimacy typically builds the framework for a more gratifying and meaningful physical relationship. When partners feel emotionally linked, it can lead to a deeper and more satisfying physical connection, promoting a sense of closeness and contentment.

6. Strengthening Commitment: Emotional closeness is intimately linked to commitment in relationships. When individuals feel strongly connected on an emotional level, they are more inclined to invest in the relationship, work through obstacles together, and prioritize the well-being and pleasure of their partner.

7. Cultivating Emotional Well-being: Emotional intimacy adds to overall emotional well-being, generating a sense of belonging, security, and satisfaction within the partnership. It offers individuals a safe area to express their real selves, leading to enhanced self-awareness and personal progress.

Overall, emotional intimacy acts as a cornerstone for creating healthy and sustainable partnerships. By developing trust, communication, empathy, and support, individuals can create a strong emotional link that supports understanding, connection, and mutual progress within their partnership.

Providing tips for fostering empathy and understanding amongst spouses

Cultivating empathy and understanding between partners is vital for building a successful and healthy relationship. Here are some methods to help cultivate these qualities:

1. Active Listening: Practice active listening by giving your companion your complete attention when they are speaking. Focus on their remarks and try to grasp their perspective without interrupting or drafting a response. Encourage children to discuss their opinions and feelings openly.

2. Express Empathy: Show empathy by acknowledging and affirming your partner's emotions. Try to understand their feelings from their point of view, even if you may not entirely relate to their experiences. Expressing empathy makes your spouse feel heard and understood.

3. Communicate Openly: Foster open communication by creating a secure and non-judgmental space for both parties to express their thoughts, worries, and emotions. Encourage each other to talk honestly and truthfully without the fear of criticism or rejection.

4. Practice Patience: Cultivate patience when your partner is encountering hardships or expressing challenging emotions. Avoid rushing to judgment or delivering unwanted advice. Instead, provide them with the time and space they need to process their feelings and thoughts at their own pace.

5. Consider Each Other's Perspectives: Attempt to see circumstances from your partner's perspective. This can help you better comprehend their feelings, motivations, and reactions. By considering their point of view, you can acquire a better feeling of empathy and compassion for their circumstances.

6. Respect limits: Respect your partner's emotional limits by recognizing when they may require space or time alone. Allow them to set limits and communicate their needs without feeling forced or overwhelmed. Respecting limits is vital for building a healthy and balanced relationship.

7. Share Vulnerabilities: Create a supportive environment where both partners feel comfortable revealing their vulnerabilities and insecurities. Encourage each other to be open and honest about their thoughts, worries, and aspirations since this can improve the emotional tie and deepen the degree of understanding between partners.

8. Practice Gratitude: Express gratitude for your partner's presence and support in your life. Acknowledge their efforts and contributions to the partnership. Gratitude can help establish a good and supportive atmosphere, developing a stronger sense of connection and understanding between couples.

By adopting these strategies into your relationship, you may create a better feeling of empathy and understanding between you and your partner, fostering a deep and lasting connection built on mutual respect, compassion, and support.

Chapter 6

Allocating Quality Time and Shared Activities

Allocating quality time and engaging in shared activities are key components of developing good relationships and fostering emotional connection. Spending meaningful moments together helps foster a deeper relationship, enhances mutual understanding, and generates enduring memories. Here are some significant benefits and tactics for properly allocating quality time and participating in shared activities:

1. Enhancing Emotional Bonding: Allocating quality time and engaging in shared activities provide an opportunity for partners, friends, or family members to bond emotionally. Meaningful conversations and shared experiences generate a sense of closeness and improve the emotional connection between persons.

2. Improving Communication: Spending quality time together encourages open and honest communication. It fosters a conducive climate for individuals to communicate their views, feelings, and worries, leading to a deeper understanding of each other's viewpoints and emotions.

3. Promoting Mutual Interests: Engaging in shared activities allows individuals to explore and enjoy common interests and hobbies. This common enthusiasm develops a sense of camaraderie and creates opportunities for mutual learning and progress within the relationship.

4. Creating Lasting Memories: Quality time spent together typically leads to the formation of cherished memories that individuals can look back on fondly. Shared experiences, whether simple or adventurous, add to a sense of nostalgia and emotional attachment that can enhance the bond between persons.

5. Alleviating Stress: Engaging in fun shared activities can help reduce stress and encourage relaxation. It provides an opportunity for individuals to unwind, have fun, and briefly escape from the responsibilities of daily life, generating a sense of emotional well-being and contentment.

6. Building empathy and awareness: Shared activities give a platform for individuals to understand one another better, boosting empathy and building a deeper awareness of each other's preferences, abilities, and limitations.

To efficiently allocate quality time and engage in shared activities, consider the following strategies:

Scheduling Regular Quality Time: Set aside particular times for shared activities and prioritize spending quality time together, whether it's a weekly date night, a weekend getaway, or a shared hobby session.

Exploring New Interests Together: Encourage each other to pursue new activities and interests that you both find appealing. This not only develops a sense of adventure but also strengthens your emotional connection through joint discovery.

Communicating Expectations: Openly share your expectations and preferences regarding the quality time you spend together. This guarantees that both individuals feel appreciated and respected, leading to a more fun and gratifying experience.

Balancing Time for Togetherness and Independence: Strive for a healthy balance between spending quality time together and leaving each other room for different activities and personal improvement. Respecting each other's need for independence produces a more harmonious and fulfilling partnership.

By prioritizing quality time and engaging in shared activities, individuals can enhance their emotional bond, expand their understanding of one another, and develop a basis for a more fulfilling and meaningful relationship.

Stressing the significance of spending quality time together

Spending quality time together is a critical element of developing strong, healthy relationships and fostering emotional closeness. In the fast-paced and demanding society we live in, it is crucial to realize the necessity of designating time for meaningful connections and shared experiences. Here are some main reasons why spending quality time together is vital for the well-being and longevity of relationships:

1. Building Emotional Connection: Quality time allows individuals to connect on a deeper emotional level. It provides an opportunity to exchange opinions, experiences, and feelings, building a stronger emotional relationship and a sense of closeness among persons.

2. Strengthening conversation: Spending quality time together facilitates open and effective conversation. It gives a forum for individuals to communicate their opinions, worries, and desires, leading to a greater understanding of each other's perspectives and promoting healthier, more meaningful connections.

3. Creating Fond Memories: Quality time spent together typically results in the formation of cherished memories. These shared memories add to a sense of nostalgia and emotional attachment, which can enhance the emotional connection and serve as a source of joy and comfort during tough times.

4. Promoting knowledge and Empathy: Regular quality time creates a greater knowledge of each other's needs, preferences, and values. It allows individuals to build empathy and compassion for their spouses, friends, or family members, leading to a more helpful and loving connection.

5. Alleviating Stress: Quality time together acts as a means to relax and unwind, providing a reprieve from the stress and obligations of regular life. Engaging in fun activities or simply spending time in each other's company can help reduce stress levels and increase emotional well-being.

6. Building Trust and Security: Consistently spending quality time together builds a sense of trust and security inside the partnership. It reassures individuals of their value and importance to their partners, strengthening the cornerstone of a healthy and rewarding bond.

7. Fostering closeness and Romance: Quality time is vital for growing closeness and fostering romance in partnerships. It provides an opportunity for couples to show affection, develop their emotional connection, and rekindle the spark that initially brought them together.

Recognizing the value of spending quality time together and deliberately pursuing meaningful interactions can considerably contribute to the overall health and durability of relationships. By making an effort to schedule dedicated time for shared activities, talks, and experiences, individuals can establish a deeper emotional connection and create a stronger, more rewarding link with their loved ones.

Suggesting joint activities to create emotional connection and closeness

Engaging in common activities is a strong approach to creating emotional connection and closeness between persons. These activities provide possibilities for connection, communication, and shared experiences that can enhance relationships. Here are some options for shared activities that might help promote emotional connection and closeness:

1. Cooking Together: Collaborating on meal preparation may be an enjoyable and intimate pastime. Try experimenting with new dishes, swapping cooking techniques, and enjoying the rewards of your effort together.

2. outside Adventures: Plan outside activities such as hiking, camping, or picnicking. Exploring nature together can promote a spirit of adventure and provide an opportunity for meaningful conversations away from the distractions of daily life.

3. Art & Crafts: Engage in creative hobbies such as painting, pottery, or creating. Expressing yourselves via art may be a therapeutic and fun method to connect on a deeper emotional level.

4. Volunteering: Participate in volunteer work or community service activities together. Contributing to a cause you both care about can enhance your friendship and provide a shared feeling of purpose and fulfillment.

5. Exercise or Yoga: Join a fitness class, go on a run, or practice yoga together. Physical activities can promote a sense of well-being and mutual support, leading to a stronger emotional connection.

6. Traveling: Plan a journey to a new destination or revisit a beloved location. Traveling together allows you to build lasting memories, share new experiences, and expand your understanding of each other's tastes and opinions.

7. Reading and Discussing: Read the same book or watch the same movie or TV series and discuss it together. Sharing your opinions and insights can lead to meaningful conversations and a greater knowledge of each other's values and interests. 8. Music and dancing: Attend a concert, play music together, or join a dancing class. Enjoying music and dancing can stimulate emotions and generate a shared sense of joy and harmony.

8. Mindfulness Practices: Practice mindfulness activities such as meditation, breathing exercises, or nature walks. These techniques can help you connect on a deeper level and enhance emotional well-being and self-awareness.

9. DIY Projects: Take on do-it-yourself projects together, such as home improvement jobs or garden projects. Working together to achieve a common objective can increase collaboration and communication, generating a sense of accomplishment and unity.

By participating in these common activities, individuals can generate possibilities for meaningful connections, communication, and understanding. These encounters can build emotional intimacy and closeness, strengthening the foundation of a successful and lasting relationship.

Chapter 7

Conflict Resolution Techniques for Strengthening Bonds

Conflict is a natural aspect of any relationship, and learning how to settle disagreements successfully can improve the relationships between persons. Utilizing constructive dispute-resolution approaches can build understanding, empathy, and mutual respect. Here are some successful conflict resolution approaches that can help establish bonds:

1. Effective Communication: Practice active listening and convey your opinions and feelings clearly and politely. Encourage your companion to do the same. Effective communication creates the framework for understanding each other's perspectives and establishing common ground.

2. Empathy and Understanding: Put yourself in your partner's shoes and try to comprehend their point of view. Cultivate empathy by acknowledging their sentiments and expressing that you understand and appreciate their position, even if you don't agree with it.

3. Maintain Calmness: Stay calm and composed during disputes. Avoid reacting abruptly or violently, as this can aggravate the problem. Instead, approach the disagreement with a level mind and a willingness to find a solution that works for both parties.

4. Use "I" Statements: Frame your issues using "I" statements to take ownership of your feelings and experiences. This technique can prevent the debate from turning into a blame game and allows for a more meaningful discussion about the issues at hand.

5. Find Common Ground: Identify areas of agreement and shared aims. Focus on identifying common ground and similar interests, which can serve as a beginning point for resolving the disagreement and strengthening your friendship.

6. Collaborative Problem-Solving: Work together to create a mutually beneficial solution. Brainstorm alternative ideas, consider each other's opinions, and be open to compromise. A collaborative approach to problem-solving can build a sense of teamwork and togetherness within the partnership.

7. Take Breaks When Needed: If the disagreement becomes strong or emotions run high, it's crucial to take a break and return to the subject when both parties are calmer. Taking time to reflect and calm off can prevent further escalation and allow for more constructive discussion and problem-solving.

8. Apologize and Forgive: Be willing to apologize when required and forgive each other for faults. Genuine apologies and forgiveness can promote healing and enhance the link by establishing a sense of understanding, compassion, and acceptance.

9. Seek Mediation if Necessary: If settling the disagreement becomes problematic, try obtaining the advice of a neutral third party, such as a counselor or therapist. Professional mediation can provide guidance and support in navigating complicated challenges and reaching mutually accepted solutions.

By using these conflict resolution tactics, individuals can manage arguments and problems in a productive and empathic manner, ultimately strengthening the links within their relationships.

Exploring effective conflict resolution tactics in relationships

Effective conflict resolution tactics are crucial for maintaining healthy and harmonious relationships. When disagreements emerge, it's crucial to approach them with empathy, understanding, and a willingness to find mutually beneficial solutions. Here are some successful dispute-resolution tactics that can help enhance relationships:

1. Active Listening: Practice active listening by listening to your partner's perspective. Show that you understand their point of view by summarizing their thoughts and feelings and affirming their emotions.

2. Maintain Respect: Respect your partner's opinions and avoid disrespectful language or behavior. Respectful communication generates a healthy climate for resolving issues and promotes mutual understanding and gratitude.

3. Express sentiments Clearly: Articulate your sentiments and worries using "I" phrases to avoid blaming or accusing your partner. Clearly expressing your emotions can assist your partner in better comprehending your perspective and feelings.

4. Find a solution: Strive for a solution that acknowledges the needs and interests of both sides. Be open to making sacrifices and finding solutions that benefit both individuals, promoting cooperation and teamwork.

5. Take Responsibility: Acknowledge your involvement in the conflict and take responsibility for any mistakes or misconceptions. Apologize when required and exhibit a desire to work towards a resolution.

6. Set limits: Establish appropriate limits to ensure both partners feel respected and heard during the dispute resolution process. Respecting each other's limits fosters a sense of safety and trust in the relationship.

7. Focus on the Present Issue: Address the precise issue at hand without bringing up prior disagreements or irrelevant grievances. Focusing on the present issue allows for a more constructive and focused resolution process.

8. Use Humor Appropriately: Employing humor can assist in alleviating tension and create a more comfortable atmosphere throughout the conflict resolution process. However, it's crucial to use comedy courteously and sensitively to avoid trivializing the circumstance.

9. Practice Patience: Be patient and empathetic during the conflict resolution process. Resolving conflicts may take time, and it's crucial to be patient and persistent in finding a settlement that satisfies both sides.

10. Seek Mediation if Needed: If resolving the problem independently becomes tough, try seeking the assistance of a neutral third party, such as a therapist or counselor. Mediation can create a supportive environment for productive conversation and help facilitate a mutually satisfying outcome.

By following these successful conflict resolution tactics, individuals can handle problems in a constructive and empathic manner, establishing a stronger and more resilient connection.

Discussing the significance of constructive conflict management

Constructive conflict management is vital for maintaining healthy and productive relationships, whether they are romantic, familial, or professional. It entails approaching problems positively and proactively to resolve issues in a way that promotes understanding, growth, and mutual respect. Here are some basic reasons why constructive conflict management is important:

1. Promotes Understanding: Constructive conflict management supports open and honest communication, allowing individuals to share their viewpoints and concerns in a safe and respectful atmosphere. This creates a greater knowledge of each other's opinions and experiences, leading to enhanced empathy and a deeper relationship.

2. Facilitates Growth and Learning: Managing disputes constructively provides a chance for self and relational growth. By positively confronting problems and differences, individuals can learn more about themselves and each other, leading to better self-awareness and improved interpersonal dynamics.

3. Strengthens Relationships: Constructive conflict management can improve the links within relationships. When problems are addressed with patience, understanding, and a willingness to find common ground, it creates trust, mutual respect, and a sense of collaboration, ultimately leading to stronger and more durable relationships.

4. Prevents Escalation of Difficulties: Addressing conflicts constructively helps prevent minor difficulties from growing into larger, more severe problems. By discussing disagreements early and efficiently, individuals can avoid extended misunderstandings and resentment, ensuring a healthier and more pleasant relationship dynamic.

5. supports Problem-Solving Skills: Constructive conflict management supports the development of competent problem-solving skills. By pursuing mutually beneficial solutions and considering the viewpoints of all parties involved, individuals can learn to approach difficulties with a solution-oriented mindset, producing a more harmonious and cooperative atmosphere.

6. Fosters a Positive atmosphere: Managing disagreements constructively adds to a positive and supportive atmosphere. By supporting open communication, understanding, and compromise, individuals can create a space where both parties feel valued, respected, and heard, leading to a more conducive and caring relationship setting.

7. Enhances Emotional Well-being: Resolving disagreements constructively can contribute to better emotional well-being. Addressing and resolving conflicts in a good manner helps lessen stress, worry, and tension, providing a sense of calm and contentment within the partnership.

Overall, constructive conflict management is vital for creating healthy, happy, and long-lasting relationships. By stressing open communication, empathy, respect, and a collaborative approach to problem-solving, individuals can develop a strong foundation for positive and sustainable interactions with others.

Chapter 8

Expressing Appreciation and Affection in Relationships

Expressing appreciation and compassion is crucial for nurturing strong and fulfilling relationships. It provides a sense of connection, closeness, and emotional well-being inside the partnership. Here are some great ways to demonstrate appreciation and admiration in relationships:

1. Verbal Affirmations: Use words to convey thanks and affection. Regularly share your gratitude for your partner, expressing praise for their qualities, acts, and contributions to the relationship.

2. Acts of Service: Show your affection by completing acts of service for your companion. This could be helping with domestic tasks, conducting errands, or providing support during hard times.

3. Quality Time: Allocate devoted time to spend together, participating in things that you both enjoy. Quality time builds a deeper emotional connection and enables meaningful conversations and shared experiences.

4. Physical Affection: Demonstrate affection by physical touch, such as hugging, holding hands, or kissing. Physical affection can transmit love, comfort, and emotional support, strengthening the link between lovers.

5. Gift-giving: Surprise your partner with meaningful presents or gestures that reflect their interests, preferences, or needs. Thoughtful presents can reflect your knowledge of their desires and enhance the emotional connection between you.

6. Encouragement and Support: Offer words of encouragement and support during both hard and successful moments. Express belief in your partner's talents and provide reassurance that you are there to support them through thick and thin.

7. Active Listening: Listen closely to your partner's thoughts and feelings without judgment. Show empathy and understanding, allowing your spouse to feel heard and appreciated in the relationship.

8. Surprises and Spontaneity: Plan surprises or spontaneous activities to add excitement and enthusiasm to the relationship. Surprise outings, romantic gestures, or spontaneous expressions of affection can inject a sense of adventure and spontaneity into the relationship.

9. Acknowledgment of work: Acknowledge and appreciate the work your partner puts into the relationship, whether it's for modest everyday duties or large life events. Recognizing their efforts can reinforce a sense of validation and gratitude in the relationship.

10. Written Communication: Express your affection through written communication, such as love notes, letters, or sincere texts. Written messages of love and admiration can serve as cherished souvenirs and reminders of the strength of your emotional relationship.

By adopting these tactics into your relationship, you can create a nurturing and supportive environment that develops appreciation, affection, and emotional closeness, ultimately deepening the link between you and your partner.

Highlighting the influence of expressing appreciation on relationship dynamics

Expressing appreciation in a relationship can have a huge positive impact on the dynamics and overall well-being of the couple. When individuals make a conscious effort to notice and express gratitude for their partner's accomplishments, efforts, and traits, it can promote a more happy and harmonious relationship. Here are some significant ways in which expressing appreciation can alter relationship dynamics:

1. Fosters Emotional Connection: Expressing appreciation increases the emotional relationship between partners. It generates a sense of closeness, understanding, and mutual respect, establishing a deeper emotional connection and intimacy within the partnership.

2. Promotes Positivity: Appreciation cultivates a pleasant attitude within the relationship. It emphasizes an emphasis on the strengths and positive traits of the partner, creating optimism and a sense of pleasure within the connection.

3. Builds Trust and Security: When individuals feel appreciated and respected, it develops a sense of trust and security within the connection. Expressing appreciation indicates a genuine acknowledgment of the partner's efforts and accomplishments, establishing a caring and nurturing environment that develops the basis of trust.

4. Encourages Reciprocity: Expressing appreciation often leads to a circle of reciprocity, where both partners are compelled to reciprocate the acts of appreciation. This circle of mutual appreciation develops a dynamic of giving and receiving, producing a more balanced and rewarding partnership.

5. Enhances conversation: Appreciation encourages open and honest conversation. It allows partners to express their sentiments, share their thanks, and communicate their wants and desires more effectively, leading to a deeper understanding of each other's viewpoints and emotions.

6. Boosts Relationship Satisfaction: Regularly expressing appreciation can significantly boost relationship satisfaction. Feeling appreciated and respected boosts the general pleasure and contentment within the relationship, contributing to a more meaningful and rewarding partnership.

7. Strengthens Resilience: When obstacles happen, a history of expressing appreciation can improve the resilience of the partnership. The foundation of thankfulness and acknowledgment can provide support during difficult times and assist partners in managing problems with a more positive and collaborative perspective.

8. Promotes Personal Growth: Expressing appreciation stimulates personal growth and development within the partnership. It stimulates individuals to continue showing positive qualities and actions, generating a sense of self-improvement and mutual support within the partnership.

By acknowledging and expressing appreciation for each other's efforts and traits, partners can establish a more positive and supportive relationship dynamic that increases emotional connection, trust, and overall pleasure within the partnership.

Discussing numerous ways to display appreciation and gratitude for your relationship

Demonstrating affection and gratitude for your partner is vital for maintaining a successful and fulfilling relationship. Showing appreciation can enhance the emotional tie, increase overall relationship satisfaction, and foster a good and supportive culture. Here are different methods to display appreciation and gratitude for your partner:

1. Vocal affirmations: Express your love and admiration through heartfelt vocal affirmations. Tell your partner how much they mean to you and constantly show your thanks for their presence in your life.

2. Acts of Service: Show your affection by completing thoughtful acts of service. Help with household chores, do errands, or aid with things that can reduce some of your partner's difficulties and duties.

3. Quality Time: Allocate devoted quality time to spend together without interruptions. Engage in activities you both enjoy, have meaningful conversations, and build lasting experiences that strengthen the emotional connection between you.

4. Physical Affection: Demonstrate affection by physical touch, such as hugs, kisses, and holding hands. Physical affection can transmit love, warmth, and emotional support, generating a stronger sense of intimacy and connection.

5. Gift-giving: Surprise your partner with meaningful presents or gestures that reflect their interests and desires. Personalized gifts or little gestures of appreciation can show your love and gratitude in a physical and meaningful way.

6. Written Communication: Express your thoughts through written communication, such as love letters, notes, or meaningful messages. Written statements of affection and thanks can serve as cherished treasures that your partner can review and enjoy over time.

7. Surprises and Spontaneity: Plan surprises or spontaneous activities to provide excitement and joy to your partner's day. Surprise outings, spontaneous expressions of affection, or intentional surprises can infuse your relationship with a sense of energy and spontaneity.

8. Active Listening: Demonstrate your affection by actively listening to your partner without judgment or interruption. Show empathy and understanding, and give a supportive environment for your spouse to share their thoughts, feelings, and concerns openly.

9. Encouragement and Support: Offer words of encouragement and support to inspire your spouse throughout both hard and successful moments. Express your belief in their skills and provide comfort that you are there to assist them through thick and thin.

10. Respect and Understanding: Show respect for your partner's beliefs, viewpoints, and boundaries. Demonstrate compassion and empathy, and aim to create a supportive and respectful environment where both partners feel valued and heard.

By combining these diverse ways of displaying affection and gratitude in your relationship, you can build a nurturing and loving environment that fosters a deep emotional connection and promotes mutual appreciation and respect.

Chapter 9

Prioritizing Self-Care and Personal Growth for Relationship Well-Being

Prioritizing self-care and personal growth is vital for maintaining overall relationship well-being. Taking care of oneself allows individuals to create a healthy and happy mindset, leading to a more meaningful and resilient connection. Here are some ways in which prioritizing self-care and personal growth might help to

1. Enhanced Emotional Well-being: Prioritizing self-care increases emotional well-being, leading to a more balanced and happy outlook. When individuals prioritize their mental and emotional health, they are better equipped to face issues within the relationship with resilience and understanding.

2. Increased Self-Awareness: Engaging in self-care techniques fosters self-awareness and introspection. Understanding one's own needs, desires, and boundaries promotes improved communication and fosters a deeper understanding of oneself and one's relationship.

3. increased Communication: Prioritizing personal improvement generally leads to increased communication abilities. As individuals work on themselves, they become more competent at communicating their thoughts, wants, and worries, resulting in more open and honest communication within the relationship.

4. Respect for Boundaries: Prioritizing self-care fosters the formation and maintenance of healthy boundaries. When individuals respect their boundaries, they are better equipped to comprehend and respect their partner's boundaries, producing a partnership dynamic centered on mutual respect and understanding.

5. Modeling Healthy Behavior: Prioritizing self-care and personal growth provides a healthy example for your partner. When both members in a relationship prioritize their well-being, they inspire each other to engage in healthy habits and behaviors, ultimately producing a more supportive and nurturing union.

6. Promotion of Mutual Support: Taking care of oneself allows people to be more present and supportive within the relationship. When individuals prioritize their personal growth, they may provide stronger support and understanding to their partner, creating a dynamic that supports reciprocal growth and well-being.

7, Reduction of Relationship Stress: Engaging in self-care activities can lessen overall relationship stress. When individuals prioritize their well-being, they are better equipped to manage stress and problems within the relationship, resulting in a more peaceful and rewarding partnership.

Encouragement of Personal Development: Prioritizing personal growth supports continuing development and learning. When individuals consistently seek to develop themselves, it contributes to a relationship dynamic that supports and fosters personal and reciprocal progress, resulting in a more meaningful and dynamic connection.

By prioritizing self-care and personal growth, individuals can establish a healthier and more supportive relationship dynamic, ultimately contributing to the overall well-being and longevity of the partnership.

Emphasizing the value of individual well-being in a relationship

Emphasizing individual well-being within a relationship is vital for creating a robust and healthy partnership. When individuals prioritize their own physical, emotional, and mental health, they contribute to the overall well-being and longevity of the relationship. Here are a few main reasons why addressing individual well-being is significant within a relationship:

1. Promotes Personal Growth: Prioritizing individual well-being stimulates personal growth and development. When individuals focus on their self-improvement, they bring a sense of fulfillment and confidence to the partnership, generating a dynamic of mutual support and encouragement.

2. Enhances Emotional Resilience: Emphasizing individual well-being helps build emotional resilience within each relationship. When individuals prioritize their emotional health, they become better equipped to face obstacles and conflicts within the relationship with patience, compassion, and empathy.

3.   Stimulates   self-reflection: Emphasizing individual well-being stimulates self-reflection and introspection. Taking the time to understand one's wants, desires, and boundaries leads to a deeper understanding of oneself and the ability to convey these aspects successfully within the relationship.

4. develops freedom: Emphasizing individual well-being develops a sense of freedom within each partner. When individuals preserve a healthy sense of self-identity and independence, they contribute to a balanced and fulfilling relationship dynamic based on mutual respect and understanding.

5. Reduces Codependency: Prioritizing individual well-being helps decrease the possibility of codependent tendencies inside the relationship. When both partners emphasize their well-being, they develop a partnership based on mutual support and encouragement rather than dependence and neediness.

6. Creates a Positive Role Model: Emphasizing individual well-being within the relationship creates a positive example for each partner. When individuals prioritize their health and happiness, they motivate their spouse to do the same, establishing a supportive and nurturing environment that supports personal growth and fulfillment.

7. Maintains a Sense of Identity: Prioritizing individual well-being helps maintain a strong sense of identity within each partner. When individuals preserve their interests, hobbies, and social contacts, they contribute to a relationship dynamic that honors and respects each other's individuality.

8. Contributes to Overall Partnership Health: Emphasizing individual well-being eventually contributes to the overall health and longevity of the partnership. When both partners prioritize their physical, emotional, and mental health, they develop a connection focused on mutual respect, support, and understanding, leading to a more rewarding and resilient bond.

By emphasizing the value of individual well-being within a relationship, individuals can establish a dynamic that supports personal growth, emotional resilience, and mutual respect, ultimately leading to a more fulfilling and durable partnership.

Providing self-care techniques to encourage personal growth and emotional resilience

Certainly, developing personal growth and emotional resilience via self-care is vital for sustaining general well-being and fostering a good outlook. Here are some self-care tips that might help individuals prioritize their personal growth and emotional resilience:

1. Prioritize Rest and Sleep: Ensure you get adequate rest and quality sleep to restore both your body and mind. Creating a consistent sleep routine and using relaxation techniques before bedtime can improve sleep quality.

2. Practice Mindfulness and Meditation: Incorporate mindfulness and meditation practices into your daily routine to increase emotional well-being and reduce stress. Taking a few moments each day to focus on your breath and be present in the moment can help build a sense of inner serenity and clarity.

3. Engage in Regular Physical Activity: Participate in regular physical activity to increase your attitude and energy levels. Whether it's a brisk stroll, yoga, or a workout session, physical activity can release endorphins and lead to a more cheerful attitude in life.

4. Nurture Healthy Eating Habits: Focus on keeping a balanced and healthy diet to promote your overall well-being. Incorporate a mix of fruits, vegetables, nutritious grains, and lean meats into your meals to enhance physical and emotional wellness.

5. Cultivate a Supportive Social Network: Foster ties with friends, family, or support groups to create a sense of belonging and emotional support. Engaging in meaningful talks and activities with loved ones can bring comfort and encouragement during tough times.

6. Set Realistic Goals: Establish feasible personal and professional goals that correspond with your values and interests. Break down major goals into smaller, attainable activities, and celebrate your victories along the way to preserve motivation and a sense of accomplishment.

7. Practice Self-Compassion: Be gentle to yourself and practice self-compassion. Acknowledge your skills and achievements, and treat yourself with the same care and understanding that you would offer to a friend facing comparable circumstances.

8. Engage in Creative Outlets: Explore creative hobbies such as painting, writing, or playing a musical instrument to express yourself and create emotional resilience. Engaging in creative hobbies can bring a sense of fulfillment and serve as a healthy outlet for processing emotions.

9. Establish limits: Set clear limits in your personal and professional life to protect your time, energy, and emotional well-being. Communicate your limits assertively and respectfully, and prioritize activities and relationships that correspond with your beliefs and aspirations.

10. Seek Professional Support: Don't hesitate to seek the help of a therapist or counselor if you are coping with emotional issues. Professional support can provide vital insights, coping skills, and resources to negotiate tough emotions and encourage personal growth and resilience.

By integrating these self-care strategies into your daily routine, you may encourage personal growth and cultivate emotional resilience, ultimately developing a more positive and rewarding attitude toward life.

Chapter 10

10. The Role of External Support in Relationship Renovation

External support can play a significant role in relationship restoration, offering valuable guidance, perspective, and resources for couples looking to enhance their relationship dynamics. Whether it's through counseling, therapy, or community support, external aid can provide a new outlook and constructive techniques to help couples negotiate obstacles and improve their bond. Here's how external help might contribute to relationship renovation:

1. Professional advice: Therapists and relationship counselors can give specialized advice and expertise to help couples address underlying issues and communication difficulties. They provide a neutral and supportive atmosphere for couples to discuss their issues, practice good communication techniques, and build strategies for resolving conflicts.

2. Mediation Services: Mediators can assist couples in resolving issues and establishing mutually beneficial solutions. They enable productive discussion and negotiation, helping couples establish common ground and work through problems fairly and courteously.

3. Educational Workshops and Seminars: Relationship workshops and seminars give couples with useful insights and tools for strengthening their communication skills and understanding each other's needs. These training programs frequently focus on creating trust, promoting intimacy, and fostering a deeper emotional connection within the relationship.

4. Support Groups: Participating in support groups or community activities for couples can bring a sense of friendship and understanding. Interacting with other couples facing similar issues can offer reassurance, empathy, and shared experiences that add to a sense of validation and support.

5. Online Resources: Accessing online resources such as articles, forums, and educational materials can give couples with vital information and self-help tools for relationship enhancement. Online tools typically offer practical techniques, exercises, and advice for encouraging better communication and tackling common relationship challenges.

6. Family and Friends: Seeking advice and support from reliable friends and family members can offer couples a different perspective on their marital issues. Having a strong support network can provide emotional validation and direction, helping couples feel more understood and supported during the restoration process.

7. Retreats and Intensive Programs: Participating in relationship retreats or intensive programs can offer couples a concentrated and immersive experience focused on revitalizing their connection and tackling key marital concerns. These programs generally involve therapeutic activities, workshops, and counseling sessions aimed to enhance emotional connection and mutual understanding.

External support can offer couples the tools and resources they need to resolve issues, increase communication, and strengthen their relationship. By obtaining external treatment, couples can gain vital insights, direction, and techniques for renovating their relationship and establishing a happier and more happy partnership.

Discussing the function of couples therapy and counseling in developing trust and love

Couples therapy and counseling play a critical part in rebuilding trust and love within a relationship that has faced obstacles or tensions. These therapeutic approaches provide an organized and supportive atmosphere for couples to address their challenges, increase communication, and work toward rebuilding trust and emotional connection. Here's a discussion on the role of couples therapy and counseling in regaining trust and love:

1. Facilitating Open Communication: Couples therapy and counseling establish a secure and neutral space for couples to interact openly and honestly. Therapists assist couples in articulating their thoughts, feelings, and worries, facilitating beneficial talks that can be difficult to conduct on their own.

2. Identifying Underlying Issues: Therapists assist couples in uncovering the underlying issues that have undermined trust and love in the relationship.

This method frequently entails evaluating prior experiences, individual traumas, communication habits, and unfulfilled needs.

3. Improving Conflict Resolution: Effective conflict resolution is a fundamental emphasis of couples therapy. Therapists educate couples on healthy and polite methods to manage disagreements and conflicts, reducing damage to trust and love during hard times.

4. Rebuilding Trust: Couples therapy gives a disciplined framework for rebuilding trust. Therapists offer tactics and exercises to help couples develop trust gradually and sustainably, emphasizing honesty, transparency, and constancy.

5. Enhancing Emotional Connection: Therapists work with couples to bond emotionally. They assist couples through activities and conversations that help them recover the emotional intimacy and affection that may have lost over time.

6. Providing Tools for Resilience: Couples therapy gives partners with tools and methods to cope with obstacles and disappointments. This involves developing emotional resilience, problem-solving abilities, and stress management approaches to better handle future difficulties.

7. Restoring Intimacy: Therapists help couples regain physical and emotional intimacy, improving their connection and affection for one another. This might involve discussions on desires, boundaries, and techniques to restart physical and emotional connections.

8. Working Toward Mutual Goals: Therapists aid couples in identifying mutual goals for the relationship. These goals may entail enhanced communication, trust-building, and increasing emotional connection. Achieving these tasks aids in reestablishing love and trust.

9. Accountability and Responsibility: Couples therapy fosters accountability for one's actions and obligations within the partnership. It helps individuals comprehend the impact of their behavior on their spouse and how personal actions contribute to rebuilding or dissolving trust and love.

10. Sustaining beneficial improvements: Couples therapy gives a framework for sustaining beneficial improvements beyond the therapy sessions. Couples learn to utilize the tools and tactics they've learned in their daily lives to ensure enduring improvements in the relationship.

Couples therapy and counseling serve as a vital resource for couples wanting to regain trust and love within their partnership. By giving professional advice, support, and a structured approach to resolving challenges and promoting emotional connection, these therapeutic methods offer a road to healing and revitalizing the partnership.

Conclusion

Building and maintaining a strong and successful relationship demands devotion, effort, and a deep knowledge of each other's needs and emotions. Throughout this conversation, we have covered several ideas and techniques that help to nurture a healthy and durable bond between couples. From prioritizing emotional closeness to boosting individual well-being and seeking external assistance, each facet plays a key part in creating a deep and lasting connection.

One of the important ideas that have developed is the significance of emotional connection in partnerships. This requires establishing open and honest communication, actively listening to one another's concerns, and demonstrating empathy and understanding. Cultivating emotional closeness gives a secure space for couples to discuss their thoughts and feelings, building a strong foundation of trust and mutual respect.

Effective communication serves as a cornerstone of any successful partnership. By practicing active listening, employing "I" statements, and maintaining a calm and courteous tone during arguments, couples can handle problems and disagreements productively. Clear and sympathetic communication develops a greater knowledge of each other's views, facilitating a more peaceful and rewarding relationship dynamic.

Allocating quality time for shared activities is another key component in strengthening emotional attachments. Engaging in activities that both partners enjoy develops a sense of unity and togetherness, producing lasting memories and establishing a deeper emotional connection. Whether it's through common hobbies, outings, or meaningful talks, spending quality time together promotes a sense of belonging and intimacy inside the partnership.

Expressing appreciation and affection acts as a powerful technique to reinforce emotional connection and mutual respect. Verbal affirmations, acts of service, physical love, and thoughtful gestures all contribute to building a nurturing and supportive environment for both partners. By praising one other's efforts and demonstrating thankfulness, couples can create a strong sense of mutual respect and love.

Furthermore, prioritizing self-care and personal well-being is vital for maintaining a strong and fulfilling relationship. By taking care of their unique needs and nurturing personal growth, individuals can contribute to a more balanced and happy union. Engaging in self-care routines, creating personal goals, and seeking support when required are key elements in fostering emotional resilience and general well-being.

In hard times, obtaining external support, such as couples therapy and counseling, can provide valuable insight and tactics for overcoming hurdles and regaining trust and love. Professional intervention offers a controlled and safe setting for couples to address underlying difficulties, increase communication, and work toward resolving disagreements. Therapists and counselors provide skills and approaches to assist couples in negotiating issues and building a deeper understanding and connection.

Overall, the route to developing a solid and durable relationship is multidimensional and takes continual effort and commitment from both partners. By building emotional closeness, prioritizing efficient communication, engaging in shared activities, and promoting individual well-being, couples can establish a supportive and nurturing atmosphere that enhances their emotional bond and cultivates a durable and happy partnership. Through mutual respect, understanding, and a willingness to grow together, couples can negotiate problems and build a relationship built on trust, love, and emotional connection.

www.ingramcontent.com/pod-product-compliance
Lightning Source LLC
Chambersburg PA
CBHW070906260726

48661CB00004B/1626